KNEELING IN BETHLEHEM

BOOKS BY ANN WEEMS
Published by The Westminster Press

Kneeling in Bethlehem

Family Faith Stories

Reaching for Rainbows:
Resources for Creative Worship

KNEELING IN BETHLEHEM

ANN WEEMS

The Westminster Press
Philadelphia

Book design by Gene Harris

First edition

Published by The Westminster Press®
Philadelphia, Pennsylvania

PRINTED IN THE UNITED STATES OF AMERICA

15   16   17   18   19

Library of Congress Cataloging-in-Publication Data

Weems, Ann, 1934–
    Kneeling in Bethlehem.

    1. Christmas—Poetry.   2. Jesus Christ—Poetry.
I. Title.
PS3573.E354K5 1987   811'.54   87-8292
ISBN 0-664-21323-5

To my children,
Stuart, Todd, David, and Heather—

In celebration of all our treks into silent December nights
in search of stars
and the wondrous times we've spent singing our joy
manger-side—

Love,
Mom

CONTENTS

ACKNOWLEDGMENTS

Grateful acknowledgment is made for permission to reprint the poems listed below, as follows:

To *A.D.* magazine, for "In Search of Our Kneeling Places," "To Listen, to Look," "Toward the Light," "Godburst," "Had We Been There," "Wouldn't It Be Grand to Be an Angel?", and "Christmas Shopping," from the Advent Calendar in the November 1981 issue.

To the Presbyterian Church (U.S.A.), for "The Gifts of the Magi," from *Abound in Hope.*

To The Westminster Press, for "Mary, Nazareth Girl," "The Refugees," "We Seem to Forget," and "God So Loved the World" from *Family Faith Stories;* and "O Lord, You Were Born!", "Christmas Comes," "Peace on Earth," "Gifts from God," "Star-giving," "The Cross in the Manger," "Christmas Trees and Strawberry Summers," and "The Church Year" from *Reaching for Rainbows.*

ADVENT

THE COMING OF GOD

Our God is the One who comes to us
    in a burning bush,
        in an angel's song,
            in a newborn child.
Our God is the One who cannot be found
    locked in the church,
    not even in the sanctuary.
Our God will be where God will be
    with no constraints,
    no predictability.
Our God lives where our God lives,
    and destruction has no power
        and even death cannot stop
            the living.
Our God will be born where God will be born,
  but there is no place to look for the One who comes to us.
When God is ready
    God will come
        even to a godforsaken place
        like a stable in Bethlehem.
Watch . . .
    for you know not when
        God comes.
Watch, that you might be found
    whenever
        wherever
            God comes.

YESTERDAY'S PAIN

Some of us walk into Advent
    tethered to our unresolved yesterdays
        the pain still stabbing
        the hurt still throbbing.
It's not that we don't know better;
    it's just that we can't stand up anymore by ourselves.
On the way to Bethlehem,
    will you give us a hand?

IN DECEMBER DARKNESS

The whole world waits in December darkness
    for a glimpse of the Light of God.
Even those who snarl "Humbug!"
    and chase away the carolers
    have been seen looking toward the skies.
The one who declared he never would forgive
    has forgiven,
  and those who left home
    have returned,
  and even wars are halted,
    if briefly,
  as the whole world looks starward.
In the December darkness
    we peer from our windows
        watching for an angel with rainbow wings
        to announce the Hope of the World.

ANGEL-FILLED ADVENT

Wouldn't it be wonderful
  if Advent came filled with angels and alleluias?
Wouldn't it be perfect
  if we were greeted on these December mornings
    with a hovering of heavenly hosts
  tuning their harps and brushing up on their fa-la-las?
Wouldn't it be incredible
  if their music filled our waking hours
    with the promise of peace on earth
  and if each Advent night we dreamed of nothing but goodwill?
Wouldn't we be ecstatic
  if we could take those angels shopping,
    or trim the tree or have them hold our hands
      and dance through our houses decorating?
And, oh, how glorious it would be
  to sit in church next to an angel
    and sing our hark-the-heralds!
What an Advent that would be!
What Christmas spirit we could have!
An angel-filled Advent has so many possibilities!
But in lieu of that,
  perhaps we can give thanks
    for the good earthly joys we have been given
      and for the earthly "angels" that we know
        who do such a good job of filling
          our Advent with alleluias!

PILGRIMAGE

IN SEARCH OF OUR KNEELING PLACES

In each heart lies a Bethlehem,
 an inn where we must ultimately answer
  whether there is room or not.
When we are Bethlehem-bound
 we experience our own advent in his.
When we are Bethlehem-bound
 we can no longer look the other way
  conveniently not seeing stars
   not hearing angel voices.
We can no longer excuse ourselves by busily
 tending our sheep or our kingdoms.

This Advent let's go to Bethlehem
 and see this thing that the Lord has made known to us.
In the midst of shopping sprees
 let's ponder in our hearts the Gift of Gifts.
Through the tinsel
 let's look for the gold of the Christmas Star.
In the excitement and confusion, in the merry chaos,
 let's listen for the brush of angels' wings.
This Advent, let's go to Bethlehem
 and find our kneeling places.

TO LISTEN, TO LOOK

Is it all sewn up—my life?
Is it at this point so predictable,
  so orderly,
    so neat,
      so arranged,
       so right,
  that I don't have time or space
    for listening for the rustle of angels' wings
    or running to stables to see a baby?
Could this be what he meant when he said
  Listen, those who have ears to hear . . .
  Look, those who have eyes to see?
O God, give me the humbleness of those shepherds
  who saw in the cold December darkness
  the Coming of Light
  the Advent of Love!

TOWARD THE LIGHT

Too often our answer to the darkness
  is not running toward Bethlehem
    but running away.
We ought to know by now that we can't see
  where we're going in the dark.
Running away is rampant . . .
  separation is stylish:
    separation from mates, from friends, from self.
Run and tranquilize,
  don't talk about it,
  avoid.
Run away and join the army
  of those who have already run away.
When are we going to learn that Christmas Peace
  comes only when we turn and face the darkness?
Only then will we be able to see
  the Light of the World.

THE BIRTH

MARY, NAZARETH GIRL

Mary,
  Nazareth girl:
What did you know of ethereal beings
  with messages from God?
What did you know of men
  when you found yourself with child?
What did you know of babies,
  you, barely out of childhood yourself?
God-chosen girl:
What did you know of God
  that brought you to this stable
  blessed among women?
Could it be that you had been ready
  waiting
    listening
      for the footsteps
    of an angel?
Could it be there are messages for us
  if we have the faith to listen?

THE CHILD IS BORN AGAIN

Each year the Child is born again.
Each year some new heart
    finally hears
        finally sees
            finally knows love.
And in heaven
    there is great rejoicing!
There is a festival of stars!
There is celebration among the angels!
For in the finding of one lost sheep,
    the heart of the Shepherd is glad, and
    Christmas has happened once more.
The Child is born anew
    and one more knee is bowed!

GODBURST

When the Holy Child is born into our hearts
    there is a rain of stars
      a rushing of angels
        a blaze of candles
    this God burst into our lives.
Love is running through the streets.

O LORD, YOU WERE BORN!

Each year about this time I try to be sophisticated
   and pretend I understand the bored expressions
      relating to the "Christmas spirit."
I nod when they say "Put the Christ back in Christmas."
I say yes, yes, when they shout "Commercial" and
      "Hectic, hectic, hectic."
After all, I'm getting older,
   and I've heard it said, "Christmas is for children."
But somehow a fa-la-la keeps creeping out. . . .
So I'll say it:
I love Christmas tinsel
   and angel voices that come from the beds upstairs.
And I say three cheers for Santa Claus
   and the Salvation Army bucket
   and all the wrappings and festivities and special warm feelings.
I say it is good,
   giving,
     praising,
       celebrating.
So hooray for Christmas trees
   and candlelight
   and the good old church pageant.
Hooray for shepherd boys who forget their lines
   and Wise Men whose beards fall off
   and a Mary who giggles.
O Lord, you were born!

O Lord, you were born!
And that breaks in upon my ordered life like bugles blaring,
   and I sing "Hark, the Herald Angels"
   in the most unlikely places.
You were born
   and I will celebrate!

I rejoice for the carnival of Christmas!
I clap for the pajama-clad cherubs
   and the Christmas cards jammed in the mail slot.
I o-o-o-oh for the turkey
   and ah-h-h-h for the Christmas pudding

and thank God for the alleluias I see in the faces of people
I don't know
   and yet know very well.

O Lord, there just aren't enough choirboys to sing what I feel.
There aren't enough trumpets to blow.
O Lord, I want bells to peal!
I want to dance in the streets of Bethlehem!
I want to sing with the heavenly host!
For unto us a Son was given
   and he was called *God with Us.*
For those of us who believe,
   the whole world is decorated in love!

THE STABLE

HOLDING

The Day is here
   and we made it to Bethlehem!
The time has come for kneeling
   and we've seen the Child!
There is singing in the stable
    and we want desperately to hold on to it . . .
   hold on to the Star!
    and the angels!
     and the spirit of love!
How do we hold on
   to the Christmas spirit?
Why can't every day be Christmas?

The world mutters "Be realistic,"
  and sometimes we church people mutter too.
On our way back from Bethlehem
  sometimes we forget
   what we've been warned about in a dream:
    to return another way.
Once we've seen the Child,
  we're left holding hearts
   wherein angels dance
    and stars sing!
Once we've been to Bethlehem,
  every day *is* Christmas!

WHAT DO I WANT FOR CHRISTMAS?

What do I want for Christmas?
I want to kneel in Bethlehem,
    the air thick with alleluias,
        the angels singing
            that God is born among us.
In the light of the Star,
    I want to see them come,
        the wise ones and the humble.
I want to see them come
    bearing whatever they treasure
        to lay at the feet
            of him who gives his life.

What do I want for Christmas?
To see in that stable
    the whole world kneeling in thanks
        for a promise kept:
            new life.
For in his nativity
    we find ours.

AGAINST OUR BETTER JUDGMENT

We told her she couldn't go;
    she was too young
        to stay up that late.
She told us that
    Baby Jesus would be there
        and he was younger than she.
We told him he couldn't go;
    he was too old
        to brave the cold night air.
He told us he'd rather greet heaven
    from the Christmas Eve service
        than be found slumped by the TV.
So we bundled them up
    against the extreme cold
    against their own defenselessness
    against our better judgment
        and they went out with joy.
My prayer is that those of us who think
    that we're in charge of the world and the church
        will remember that the stable was filled
            with such as these:
    those who could not be kept
        from rejoicing!

HAD WE BEEN THERE

Into the stable they straggled, poor and dirty,
hardly suitably dressed for polite society.
Had we been Joseph
we would have feared robbery.
Had we been Mary
we would have feared germs around our newborn.
Had we been God
these are not ones we would have chosen
to first come and see the Child.
After all, they showed a certain carelessness
about the rules of the church.
And yet, God-chosen, they came
to kneel and worship him
whom we would later call the Good Shepherd.
Perhaps we could brush up on our humbleness.

ANGELS

THIS YEAR

I wonder if God comes to the edge of heaven each Advent
   and flings the Star into the December sky,
      laughing with joy as it lights the darkness of the earth;
   and the angels, hearing the laughter of God,
      begin to congregate in some celestial chamber
         to practice their alleluias.
I wonder if there's some ordering of rank among the angels
   as they move into procession,
      the seraphim bumping the cherubim from top spot,
      the new inhabitants of heaven standing in the back
         until they get the knack of it.
(After all, treading air over a stable and annunciating at the
   same time can't be all that easy!)
Or is everybody—that is, every "soul"—free to fly
   wherever the spirit moves?
Or do they even think about it?
Perhaps when God calls, perhaps they just come,
   this multitude of heavenly hosts.
Perhaps they come,
   winging through the winds of time
      full of expectancy
      full of hope
   that this year
      perhaps this year
      (perhaps)
   the earth will fall to its knees
      in a whisper of "Peace."

WOULDN'T IT BE GRAND TO BE AN ANGEL?

Wouldn't it be grand to be an angel
   and have as your address
   "The Realms of the Glory of God"?
And swing on rainbows,
   and gather stars in your pockets,
   winging in and out of earth
   in a flurry of moondust
   with the messages of God?
Comforting the distressed, warning the righteous,
   delivering the just, guarding little children?
Of course, we can comfort and warn
   and deliver and guard.
Maybe, if we get that right,
   we can swing on rainbows later.

THE CRECHE

THE PLASTIC ANGEL

Our crèche set came complete with stable
  and a plastic angel.
Small, not at all to scale,
    the white-garbed creature with uncertain wings
      was obviously an afterthought,
        thrown in to complete the set,
          otherwise ceramic and hand-painted. . . .
Unless, of course, this angel was a last-minute substitute
  for one which was irresistible to the packer.
In that case, somewhere I have an irresistible ceramic angel,
  dressed gloriously in red,
    kneeling or flying on somebody else's coffee table
      even now
        as I unwrap the plastic angel.
If I could ever bring myself to throw away an angel,
  it would be this one,
    this one with no redeeming features.
And yet, each year as I unwrap the plastic angel,
  I hesitate again to pitch this celestial messenger.
I'm reminded of my own lack of glory,
  my own plastic attempts at celebrating Christmas,
    my own feeble annunciations,
      and once again I place this bit of plastic
      over the stable.
If the plastic angel
  can get this far,
    perhaps there's a place in Bethlehem town
      for me.

IN CELEBRATION OF HIS BIRTH

Her wrinkled hands touched the tree
                  lovingly
  as though she held eighty Christmases in a touch.
And then she turned to us and smiled
                  joyfully
  and thanked us that she was here now,
    celebrating with us the birth of her Lord.
Turning again to the tree, she drew from her bag
                  carefully
  the gifts that she offered,
    and bending slightly, she placed them under the tree.
No gold, no frankincense, no myrrh
  were greater gifts than hers
  who gave all that she had
    in celebration of his birth.

UNEXPECTED

Even now we simply do not expect
    to find a deity in a stable.
Somehow the setting is all wrong:
   the swaddling clothes too plain,
   the manger too common for the likes of a Savior,
   the straw inelegant,
   the animals, reeking and noisy,
   the whole scene too ordinary for our taste.
And the cast of characters is no better.
With the possible exception of the kings,
    who among them is fit for this night?
   the shepherds? certainly too crude,
   the carpenter too rough,
   the girl too young.
And the baby!
Whoever expected a baby?
Whoever expected the advent of God in a helpless child?
Had the Messiah arrived in the blazing light of the glory
    of a legion of angels wielding golden swords,
   the whole world could have been conquered for Christ
   right then and there
   and we in the church—to say nothing of the world!—
   wouldn't have so much trouble today.
Even now we simply do not expect
    to face the world armed with love.

FAITH

CHRISTMAS MIRACLE

There are those who scoff at miracles.
I don't know what they make of the birth of the Child.
For that matter,
    I don't know what they make of the birth of any child.

There are those who laugh at dreams,
    so they've never heard an angel's voice,
    nor seen any unusual light in the night's sky,
    nor felt the yearning to set out in search
        of new life.

There are those who do not see the Star.
I wonder where it is they go
    when everyone else sets out for Bethlehem.
To those of us who believe,
    into every night is born a Star.

GETTING TO THE FRONT OF THE STABLE

Who put Joseph in the back of the stable?
Who dressed him in brown, put a staff in his hand,
 and told him to stand in the back of the crèche,
 background for the magnificent light of the Madonna?

God-chosen, this man Joseph was faithful
 in spite of the gossip in Nazareth,
 in spite of the danger from Herod.
This man, Joseph, listened to angels
 and it was he who named the Child
 Emmanuel.
Is this a man to be stuck for centuries
 in the back of the stable?
Actually, Joseph probably stood in the doorway
 guarding the mother and child
 or greeting shepherds and kings.
When he wasn't in the doorway,
 he was probably urging Mary to get some rest,
 gently covering her with his cloak,
 assuring her that he would watch the Child.
Actually, he probably picked the Child up in his arms
 and walked him in the night,
 patting him lovingly
 until he closed his eyes.

This Christmas, let us give thanks to God
 for this man of incredible faith
 into whose care God placed the Christ Child.
As a gesture of gratitude,
 let's put Joseph in the front of the stable
 where he can guard and greet
 and cast an occasional glance
  at this Child
   who brought us life.

THE CHRISTMAS SPIRIT

The Christmas spirit
    is that hope
        which tenaciously clings
            to the hearts of the faithful
  and announces
    in the face
        of any Herod the world can produce
        and all the inn doors slammed in our faces
        and all the dark nights of our souls
that with God
    all things still are possible,
that even now
    unto us
        a Child is born!

INTO THIS SILENT NIGHT

Into this silent night
    as we make our weary way
      we know not where,
just when the night becomes its darkest
    and we cannot see our path,
just then
    is when the angels rush in,
      their hands full of stars.

THE WORLD
STILL KNOWS

THE WORLD STILL KNOWS

The night is still dark
   and a procession of Herods still terrorize the earth,
      killing the children to stay in power.
The world still knows its Herods,
   but it also still knows men and women
      who pack their dreams safely in their hearts
   and set off toward Bethlehem,
      faithful against all odds,
         undeterred by fatigue or rejection,
                    to kneel to a child.

And the world still knows those persons
   wise enough
      to follow a star,
   those who do not consider themselves too intelligent
      too powerful
      too wealthy
                    to kneel to a child.

And the world still knows those hearts so humble
   that they're ready
      to hear the word of a song
         and to leave what they have, to go
                    to kneel to a child.

The night is still dark,
   but by the light of the star,
      even today
         we can still see
                    to kneel to a child.

THE DECREE

And in these days a decree goes out to all the world,
   for these are taxing times.
We are all called again to go to Bethlehem,
   no matter the state of our health or our world.
We come, obedient and faithful,
     for we have heard the message,
       we have dreamed the dream
         that God will come to dwell among us.
We come, expectant with joy,
   pregnant with anticipation,
     for God has done great things for us.
We come searching for a sign;
   bearing our gifts, we come.
We come, called from the silent hillsides of our hearts,
   startled and frightened by the magnitude of light,
     we huddle together toward Bethlehem.
We come, one by one,
   and yet, as one,
     dancing into the Promise.

SITTING ON THE HILLSIDES

Most of us who gather in Bethlehem on this night
  are not the star seekers.
We've not traveled our dreams
  month after month and year after year,
    poring over predictions and promises.
Most of us sit on our hillsides
  tending our sheep,
    business as usual.
Oh, we've heard rumors of stars,
  but we don't really give ourselves to seeking.
After all, there's more than enough to do
  in the daily tending.
We're simply not on the lookout for stars,
  nor expecting any light in our darkness.
I suppose the important thing is,
  in the light of the glory of the Lord,
    to recognize the voice of an angel
      and to get up,
        and in spite of our sheep
          to go even unto Bethlehem
            to see this thing that has happened.

NOT CELEBRATE?

Not celebrate?
Your burden is too great to bear?
Your loneliness is intensified during this Christmas season?
Your tears seem to have no end?
Not celebrate?
You should lead the celebration!
You should run through the streets
    to ring the bells and sing the loudest!
You should fling the tinsel on the tree,
    and open your house to your neighbors,
        and call them in to dance!
For it is you above all others
    who know the joy of Advent.
It is unto you that a Savior is born this day,
    One who comes to lift your burden from your shoulders,
    One who comes to wipe the tears from your eyes.
You are not alone,
    for he is born this day to you.

THE REFUGEES

Into the wild and painful cold of the starless winter night
    came the refugees,
  slowly making their way to the border.
The man, stooped from age or anxiety,
  hurried his small family through the wind.
Bearded and dark, his skin rough and cracked from the cold,
  his frame looming large in spite of the slumped shoulders:
He looked like a man who could take care of whatever
    came at them
    from the dark.
Unless, of course, there were too many of them.
One man he could handle . . . two, even . . . ,
    but a border patrol . . .
  they wouldn't have a chance.
His eyes, black and alert,
  darted from side to side, then over his shoulder,
    then back again forward.
Had they been seen?
Had they been heard?
Every rustle of wind, every sigh from the child,
  sent terror through his chest.
Was this the way?
Even the stars had been unkind—
  had hidden themselves in the ink of night
    so that the man could not read their way.
Only the wind . . . was it enough?
Only the wind and his innate sense of direction. . . .
What kind of a cruel judgment would that be,
  to wander in circles through the night?
Or to safely make their way to the border
  only to find the authorities waiting for them?
He glanced at the young woman, his bride.
No more than a child herself,
  she nuzzled their newborn, kissing his neck.
She looked up, caught his eye, and smiled.
Oh, how the homelessness had taken its toll on her!

Her eyes were red, her young face lined,
  her lovely hair matted from inattention,
    her clothes stained from milk and baby,
      her hands chapped from the raw wind of winter.
She'd hardly had time to recover from childbirth
  when word had come that they were hunted,
    and they fled with only a little bread,
      the remaining wine,
    and a very small portion of cheese.
Suddenly, the child began to make small noises.
The man drew his breath in sharply;
  the woman quietly put the child to breast.
Fear . . . long dread-filled moments. . . .
Huddled, the family stood still in the long silence.
At last the man breathed deeply again,
  reassured they had not been heard.
And into the night continued
  Mary and Joseph and the Babe.

CHRISTMAS COMES

Christmas comes every time we see God in other persons.
The human and the holy meet in Bethlehem
    or in Times Square,
  for Christmas comes like a golden storm on its way
    to Jerusalem—
determinedly, inevitably. . . .
Even now it comes
  in the face of hatred and warring—
    no atrocity too terrible to stop it,
    no Herod strong enough,
    no hurt deep enough,
    no curse shocking enough,
    no disaster shattering enough.
For someone on earth will see the star,
    someone will hear the angel voices,
    someone will run to Bethlehem,
    someone will know peace and goodwill:
    the Christ will be born!

PEACE ON EARTH

"Peace on earth, goodwill to all" . . .
The song came out like one loud hosanna
   hurled through the earth's darkness,
   lighting the Bethlehem sky.
Sometimes I hear it now,
   but it means a baby in a manger;
   it means a time of year,
   a cozy feeling,
   a few coins in the Salvation Army bucket.
It doesn't mean much—
   and then it's gone,
   lost in the tinsel.

Where did the angels' song go?
Who hushed the alleluias?
Was it death and war and disease and poverty?
Was it darkness and chaos and famine and plague?
Who brought violence and took away the sweet plucking
   of heavenly harps?
Who brought despair and took away hope?
Who brought barrenness and crushed the flowers?
Who stole the music and brought the silence?
What Herods lurk within our world seeking to kill our children?
Are there still those
   who listen for the brush of angel wings
   and look for stars above some godforsaken little stable?

Are there still those
   who long to hear an angel's song
   and touch a star?
To kneel beside some other shepherd
   in the hope of catching a glimpse of eternity in a baby's smile?
Are there still those who sing
   "Peace on earth, goodwill to all"?
If there are—then, O Lord,
   keep ablaze their flickering candle
   in the darkness of this world!

KEEPING CHRISTMAS

THIS YEAR WILL BE DIFFERENT

Who among us does not have dreams
    that this year will be different?
Who among us does not intend to go
    peacefully, leisurely, carefully toward Bethlehem,
  for who among us likes to cope with the
    commercialism of Christmas
  which lures us to tinsel not only the tree
    but also our hearts?
Who among us intends to get caught up in tearing around
    and wearing down?
Who among us does not long for:
  gifts that give love?
  shopping in serenity?
  cards and presents sent off early?
  long evenings by the fireside with those we love?
  (the trimming devoid of any arguing about who's going to hang
    what where,
  the aroma of cinnamon and nutmeg mingling with the pine
    scent of the tree,
  and carols gently playing over our idyllic scene)
  and the children! the children cheerfully talking about
    giving instead of getting?
Who among us does not yearn for
  time for our hearts to ponder the Word of God?
  moments of kneeling and bursts of song?
  the peace of quiet calm for our spirit's journey?

This year we intend to follow the Star
    instead of the crowd.
But, of course, we always do
    intend the best.
(And sometimes best intentions tend to get the best of us!)
This year, when we find ourselves off the path again
    (and we invariably will!),
  let's not add yet another stress to our Advent days,
    that of "trying to do Christmas correctly"!
Instead, let's approach the birth of our Lord
    with *joyful* abandon!

And this year
    let's do what Mary did and rejoice in God,
    let's do what Joseph did and listen to our dreams,
    let's do what the Wise Men did and go to worship,
    let's do what the shepherds did and praise and glorify God
        for all we've seen and heard!
As for the Advent frantic pace, we don't have time for that.
We'll be too busy singing!
This year will be different!

GIVING

I gave my mother Evening in Paris,
   sixty-five cents at the five-and-dime,
     a Christmas Special.
Everybody knew—in the second grade—
   that ladies longed for perfume.
I wanted to give her something special . . .
   no Christmas chocolates she'd share with the others,
   no crayoned creation to hang in the kitchen,
   no photo of me with a snaggled-tooth grin,
   but a gift that no one else would use,
     a present just for my mother.
I wrapped it in tissue
   adorned with red reindeer
and wrote "I LOVE YOU!"
   and signed it in cursive.
I thought it was the grandest gift anybody could give.
She thought so, too.

THE GIFTS OF THE MAGI

O Lord, I'd like to go to the stable this night!
I'd run
    even through the dark
        to lay my gifts at your feet!

Lord, why couldn't I have been there?
I needn't have been a king,
    perhaps just a shepherd child
        or someone sent from the inn
        to check on the progress of the birth. . . .

Or are you waiting this night in other stables
    for me
        to bring my gift?
Are you waiting for me to run
    even through the dark and cold of the night?

CHRISTMAS SHOPPING

I had a dream that the Holy Family
  came down the escalators at Field's.
Angels in red raiment flew around
  sprinkling us with stardust,
  singing alleluias and playing their bugles,
  and all the shoppers knelt in adoration and praise.
The Wise Men, working in gift wrap,
  began receiving our hearts
  and wrapped them in rainbow papers
  and we presented them to the Christ Child.
Then they were gone
  and we returned to our shopping.
But I heard no more complaining about the long lines
  and I saw no more rushing about.
We all smiled and greeted one another with
  PEACE and GOODWILL.
We all remembered we had given away our hearts.
It was the best Christmas shopping I'd ever done!

GIFTS FROM GOD

The steadfast love of the Lord never ceases;
   God's mercies never come to an end.
They are new every morning.

The Lord God gave the peoples of the earth a garden,
   and the people said, "That's very nice, God, but that's not
     enough. We'd like a little knowledge, please."
The Lord God gave them knowledge,
   and the people said, "Now that we have knowledge,
     we'd like things."
The Lord God gave the people things,
   but they always said, "That's not quite enough."
So the Lord God gave them gifts unequaled:
     the sun
     lightning and thunder
     rain and flowers
     animals and birds and fish
     trees and stars and the moon.
God gave them the rainbow.
God parted the Red Sea and gave them manna.
God gave them prophets
     and children
     and each other,
   but still the people said, "That's not quite enough."
God loved the people,
   and out of ultimate merciful goodness
   God gave them the Gift of Gifts,
   a Christmas present never to be forgotten.
God gave them love
   in the form of God's Son,
   even Christ Jesus.

There are some that don't open their eyes or their ears
     or their hearts
   and they still say, that's not quite enough.
They wander through the stores looking for Christmas.
But others open their whole being to the Lord,
   bending their knees to praise God,
   carrying Christmas with them every day.
For these the whole world is a gift!

STAR-GIVING

What I'd really like to give you for Christmas
   is a star. . . .
Brilliance in a package,
   something you could keep in the pocket of your jeans
   or in the pocket of your being.
Something to take out in times of darkness,
   something that would never snuff out nor tarnish,
   something you could hold in your hand,
   something for wonderment,
   something for pondering,
   something that would remind you of
   what Christmas has always meant:
   God's Advent Light into the darkness of this world.
But stars are only God's for giving,
   and I must be content to give you words and wishes and
     packages without stars.
But I can wish you life
   as radiant as the Star
   that announced the Christ Child's coming,
   and as filled with awe as the shepherds who stood
   beneath its light.
And I can pass on to you the love
   that has been given to me,
   ignited countless times by others
   who have knelt in Bethlehem's light.
Perhaps, if you ask, God will give you a star.

THE MESSAGE OF CHRISTMAS

WE SEEM TO FORGET

What concerns me,
   what lies on my heart,
      is this:
That we in the church
     papered and programmed
     articulate and agenda-ed
   are telling the faith story
     all wrong,
   are telling it as though it happened two thousand
     years ago
   or is going to happen
     as soon as the church budget is raised.
We seem to forget that Christ's name is Emmanuel,
  God with Us,
Not just when he sat among us
   but *now,*
   when we cannot feel the nailprints in his hands.

GOD SO LOVED THE WORLD

The story of Jesus Christ is this:
The people of this earth waited for a Messiah . . . a Savior . . .
   and only God would send a little baby king.
The child grew and began to question things as they were,
   and the man moved through his days and through this world,
     questioning the system of kings and priests and marketplace.
He was called the New Creation
         the New Covenant
         the Son of God
  who brought to all who listened
         who saw
         who understood
  change and new life.
But kings and corporations and churches of this world
   work very hard
to keep things as they are out into forever AMEN.
And so they killed him:
         he who said, Love one another,
         he who said, Feed my sheep,
  for they didn't want to share their bread and their wine.
Now the story should have ended there
   except that the story has always been
     that our God is the God of the covenant.
The Good News is that
   in spite of our faithlessness
     God is faithful
  and Jesus Christ was resurrected,
     for God so loved the world
       that God gave his only begotten Son
         that whoever believed
           might have everlasting Life.
Listen, you who have ears to hear.
Listen, and sit down to bread and wine with strangers.
Feed his sheep. . . . Love one another,
  and claim new life in his name.

THE CROSS IN THE MANGER

If there is no cross in the manger,
  there is no Christmas.
If the Babe doesn't become the Adult,
  there is no Bethlehem star.
If there is no commitment in us,
  there are no Wise Men searching.
If we offer no cup of cold water,
  there is no gold, no frankincense, no myrrh.
If there is no praising God's name,
  there are no angels singing.
If there is no spirit of alleluia,
  there are no shepherds watching.
If there is no standing up, no speaking out, no risk,
  there is no Herod, no flight into Egypt.
If there is no room in our inn,
  then "Merry Christmas" mocks the Christ Child,
  and the Holy Family is just a holiday card,
  and God will loathe our feasts and festivals.

For if there is no reconciliation,
  we cannot call Christ "Prince of Peace."
If there is no goodwill toward others,
  it can all be packed away in boxes for another year.
If there is no forgiveness in us,
  there is no cause for celebration.
If we cannot go now even unto Golgotha,
  there is no Christmas in us.
If Christmas is not *now*,
  if Christ is not born into the everyday present,
  then what is all the *noise* about?

CHRISTMAS TREES AND STRAWBERRY SUMMERS

What I'd really like is a life of Christmas trees and strawberry
    summers,
A walk through the zoo with a pocketful of bubble gum and a
    string of balloons.
I'd say "yes" to blueberry mornings and carefree days
    with rainbow endings.
I'd keep the world in springtime and the morning glories
    blooming.
But life is more than birthday parties;
  life is more than candied apples.

I'd rather hear the singing than the weeping.
I'd rather see the healing than the violence.
I'd rather feel the pleasure than the pain.
I'd rather know security than fear.
I'd like to keep the cotton candy coming.
But life is more than fingers crossed;
  life is more than wishing.

Christ said, "Follow me."
And, of course, I'd rather not.
I'd rather pretend that doesn't include me.
I'd rather sit by the fire and make my excuses.
I'd rather look the other way,
  not answer the phone,
  and be much too busy to read the paper.

But I said *yes* and
  that means risk—
  it means, Here I am, ready or not!

O Christmas trees and strawberry summers,
you're what I like and you are real.
But so are hunger
  and misery
    and hate-filled red faces.
So is confrontation.
So is injustice.
Discipleship means sometimes it's going to rain in my face.

But when you've been blind and now you see,
    when you've been deaf and now you hear,
    when you've never understood and now you know,
    once you know who God calls you to be,
    you're not content with sitting in corners.
There's got to be some alleluia shouting,
        some speaking out
        some standing up
        some caring
        some sharing
        some community
        some risk.
Discipleship means living what you know.
Discipleship means "Thank you, Lord"
    for Christmas trees and strawberry summers
    and even for rain in my face.

THE CHURCH YEAR

The church is Advent.
The unwrapping of God's greatest gift is near.
Advent—coming.
God will take away the tinsel
    and decorate our human hearts in hope
    so that Christians can sit laughing in the rain,
    knowing that the Lord is going to
        shine in upon their being.
For no matter how long the darkness,
    God will send the Light.
In spite of cursing and violence and the massacring of human
        dignity,
    we will dance in the streets of Bethlehem,
    for He will be born!

The church is Epiphany.
We are the Magi, searching,
    resplendent in this world's accouterments
    of knowledge and wealth and achievement.
But we search for something more.
And—of all unlikely places—
    in a stable
    the Deity appears.
The borning of our Lord
    bursts in upon our ordinary lives
    like fireworks in the snow.
Only God would send a little baby King,
    and we are on our knees,
    where we are within reach of our full personhood.

The church is Good Friday.
Darkness burnt into blackness,
    abysmal absence of anything good.
We acknowledge that death is real
    and we tremble for a world that would kill its God.
Our feet stand in quicksand;
    our voices echo sterile silence.
We huddle together to meet the dark and the death,
    forgetting what was taught us,

forgetting that somewhere
    a seed is sprouting,
somewhere
    a child is growing.
All we see is Christ crucified.

The church is Easter.
Out of Death: Life.
Out of darkness:
    a lush green world
    flowers in the ice
    sunrays in the storm
    mustard seeds galore.
Our souls enter a spiritual springtime,
    our bodies given over to leaping and dancing,
    our very beings saturated in hosannas.
Our shouting crashes in upon this world:
    the Lord lives!
    we live!
Resurrection resounds throughout our community.

The church is Pentecost.
The Holy Spirit is poured out upon us
    and sends us out together
        aflame with new life,
    inheritors of the wealth of God:
        life abundant.
We are liberated from the prisons of pettiness,
        jealousy, and greed,
    liberated to be the church.

We are freed to free others.
We are affirmed to affirm others.
We are loved to love others.
We are family;
    we are community.
We are the church triumphant—
    you, me, anyone who would come unto the Lord—
    renewed, redirected, empowered
    to change things and lives
    together in love and wholeness.
We are the Lord's church,
    the church of justice and mercy,

the people sent to open prisons,
                    to heal the sick
                    to clothe the naked
                    to feed the hungry
                    to reconcile
        to be alleluias when there is no music.
The mantle is upon our shoulders.
Joy is apparent in our living.
We have been commissioned to be the church of Jesus Christ.

IT IS NOT OVER

IT IS NOT OVER

It is not over,
   this birthing.
There are always newer skies
   into which
      God can throw stars.
When we begin to think
   that we can predict the Advent of God,
   that we can box the Christ
      in a stable in Bethlehem,
   that's just the time
      that God will be born
   in a place we can't imagine and won't believe.
Those who wait for God
   watch with their hearts and not their eyes,
      listening
         always listening
            for angel words.

LATER

Later
after the angels,
after the stable,
after the Child,
they went back . . .
as we always must,
back to the world that doesn't understand
our talk of angels and stars
and especially not the Child.
We go back complaining that it doesn't last.
They went back singing praises to God!
We do have to go back,
but we can still sing the alleluias!

BOXED

I must admit to a certain guilt
   about stuffing the Holy Family into a box
      in the aftermath of Christmas.
It's frankly a time of personal triumph when,
   each Advent's eve, I free them (and the others)
      from a year's imprisonment
         boxed in the dark of our basement.
Out they come, one by one,
   struggling through the straw,
      last year's tinsel still clinging to their robes.
Nevertheless, they appear,
   ready to take their place again
      in the light of another Christmas.
The Child is first
   because he's the one I'm most reluctant to box.
Attached forever to his cradle, he emerges,
   apparently unscathed from the time spent upside down
      to avoid the crush of the lid.
His mother, dressed eternally in blue,
   still gazes adoringly,
      in spite of the fact that
         her features are somewhat smudged.
Joseph has stood for eleven months,
   holding valiantly what's left of his staff,
      broken twenty Christmases ago
         by a child who hugged a little too tightly.
The Wise Ones still travel,
   though not quite so elegantly,
      the standing camel having lost its back leg
      and the sitting camel having lost one ear.
However, gifts intact, they are ready to move.
The shepherds, walking or kneeling,
   sometimes confused with Joseph
      (who wears the same dull brown),
      tumble forth, followed by three sheep
         in very bad repair.

There they are again,
    not a grand set surely,
        but one the children (and now the grandchildren)
           can touch and move about to reenact that silent night.
When the others return,
    we will wind the music box on the back of the stable
      and light the Advent candles
        and go once more to Bethlehem.
And this year, when it's time to pack the figures away,
    we'll be more careful that the Peace and Goodwill
      are not also boxed for another year!

INDEX OF FIRST LINES